little Blessings®

QUESTIONS from little hearts

Kathleen Long Bostrom
Illustrated by Elena Kucharik

FOUNDATION

Foundation Books
ORONO, ON CANADA

Edited by Betty Free Swanberg
Designed by Catherine Bergstrom

ISBN 1-894451-04-X

Printed in Italy

07 06 05 04 03
10 9 8 7 6 5 4 3 2 1

What Is God Like?

I can't see you, God,

so please give me a clue:

Do you look like me,

and do I look like you?

Are you big or little?

Are you short or tall?

Can you really see me

when I am so small?

Do you like to whisper?

Do you like to shout?

Can you sing or whistle?

I'd like to find out.

Are you strong or gentle?

Are you ever sad?

Do you have a temper

like me when I'm mad?

Where do you live?

In a house in the sky?

How do I know

you are somewhere nearby?

Do you love me always,

or just when I'm good?

I don't always do things

the way that I should.

I have lots of questions
to ask you like these.
I wonder if maybe
you'll answer them, please?

You're looking for answers?

Then here's what to do:

Just turn to the Bible

to find what is true,

And listen to everything

I say to you.

BIBLE
A-2
007

You won't find a picture

of me in a book.

There isn't one person

who knows how I look.

But don't be upset

that you can't see my face.

You can look at my work

in this beautiful place!

I've been alive
since before time began;
I made the whole world
by my very own plan.

I'm as tall as the heavens;

I'm as wide as the sea.

But even your hairs

are all counted by me.

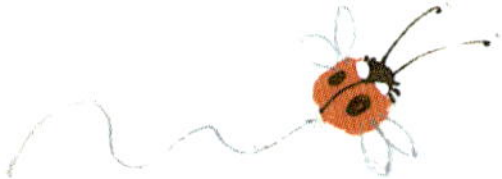

My voice can be gentle

and silent and still,

And also like thunder

that roars through the hills.

I sing with the waves

and the whistling breeze,

And joining my song

are the hills and the trees.

I'm strong as a fortress,

a rock, and a shield,

But as gentle as rain

falling softly on fields.

When you are unhappy

that makes me feel sad.

I'm filled with great joy

when I make your heart glad.

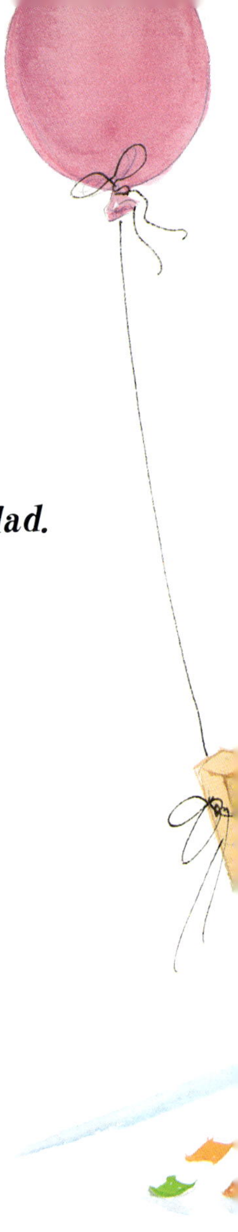

My anger comes slowly

and fades like the night.

There's no darkness in me,

just goodness and light.

I live in the world

and in heaven above.

I live in the hearts

of my people who love.

For I AM the maker
of heaven and earth.
I spoke, and my Word
brought all life into birth.

I AM like a mother

who comforts your fears

And tenderly wipes away

all of your tears.

PUPPY
CHUNKS

I AM like a father

who wants to provide,

To care for your needs

and to stay by your side.

I AM the Creator,

the first and the last,

I'm God of the present,

the future, the past.

JUNE

I AM the good shepherd,

who cares for each lamb.

I AM the Almighty,

I AM WHO I AM.

Elena

I'll love you forever,

whatever you do,

For nothing can separate

my love from you.

I've loved everything

that I made from the start.

My world and my people

I hold in my heart.

Bible References

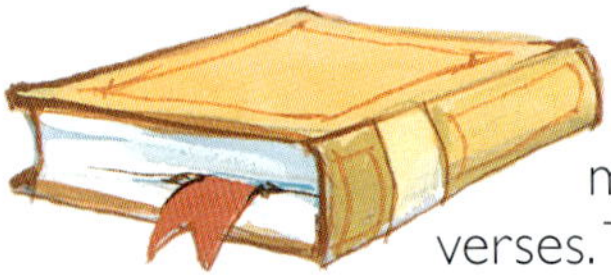

Here are some Bible verses to talk about as you read this book again with your child. You may want to open your Bible as you read the verses. This will help your little one understand that God's answers in this poem come from his Word, the Bible.

You won't find a picture of me in a book.
There isn't one person who knows how I look.

No one has ever seen God. 1 JOHN 4:12

But don't be upset that you can't see my face.
You can look at my work in this beautiful place!

Then God looked over all he had made, and he saw that it was excellent in every way. GENESIS 1:31

I've been alive since before time began;
I made the whole world by my very own plan.

In the beginning God created the heavens and the earth. GENESIS 1:1

I'm as tall as the heavens; I'm as wide as the sea.

The sky is no limit for God. . . . God's greatness is broader than the earth, wider than the sea. JOB 11:8-9, TEV

But even your hairs are all counted by me.

And the very hairs on your head are all numbered.
MATTHEW 10:30

My voice can be gentle and silent and still,

And after the fire there was the sound of a gentle whisper. 1 KINGS 19:12

And also like thunder that roars through the hills.

Listen carefully to the thunder of God's voice as it rolls from his mouth. JOB 37:2

I sing with the waves and the whistling breeze,
And joining my song are the hills and the trees.

The voice of the Lord is heard on the seas;
the glorious God thunders,
and his voice echoes over the ocean.
The Lord's voice shakes the oaks
and strips the leaves from the trees.
PSALM 29:3, 9, TEV

Let the rivers clap their hands in glee!
Let the hills sing out their songs of joy.
PSALM 98:8

You live in joy and peace. The mountains and hills will burst into song, and the trees of the field will clap their hands!
ISAIAH 55:12

I'm as strong as a fortress, a rock, and a shield,

The Lord is my protector;
he is my strong fortress . . .
He protects me like a shield;
he defends me and keeps me safe.
PSALM 18:2, TEV

You have turned from the God who can save you—the Rock who can hide you. ISAIAH 17:10

But as gentle as rain falling softly on fields.

He will respond to us as surely as the arrival of dawn or the coming of rains in early spring. HOSEA 6:3

When you are unhappy, that makes me feel sad.

The Lord is near to those who are discouraged;
he saves those who have lost all hope.
PSALM 34:18, TEV

I'm filled with great joy when I make your heart glad.

Find out for yourself how good the Lord is.
Happy are those who find safety with him.
PSALM 34:8, TEV

You have put gladness in my heart. PSALM 4:7, NRSV

My anger comes slowly and fades like the night.

The Lord is slow to anger and rich in unfailing love.
NUMBERS 14:18

There's no darkness in me, just goodness and light.

God is light and there is no darkness in him at all.
1 JOHN 1:5

I live in the world and in heaven above.

There is no one like the Lord our God.
He lives in the heights above,
but he bends down
to see the heavens and the earth.
PSALM 113:5-6, TEV

I live in the hearts of my people who love.

God is love, and all who live in love live in God, and God lives in them. I JOHN 4:16

For I AM the maker of heaven and earth.
I spoke, and my Word brought all life into birth.

The Lord merely spoke,
    and the heavens were created.
He breathed the word,
    and all the stars were born.
For when he spoke, the world began!
    It appeared at his command.
    PSALM 33:6, 9

I AM like a mother who comforts your fears

You will be like a child that is nursed by its mother, carried in her arms, and treated with love. I will comfort you . . . as a mother comforts her child. ISAIAH 66:12-13, TEV

And tenderly wipes away all of your tears.

And God will wipe away all their tears. REVELATION 7:17

I AM like a father who wants to provide,

Your heavenly Father already knows all your needs, and he will give you all you need from day to day.
MATTHEW 6:32-33

To care for your needs and to stay by your side.

I will not be afraid,
for you are close beside me.
PSALM 23:4

I AM the Creator, the first and the last.
I'm God of the present, the future, the past.

"I am the . . . beginning and the end," says the Lord God. "I am the one who is, who always was, and who is still to come, the Almighty One." REVELATION 1:8

I AM the good shepherd, who cares for each lamb.

The Lord is my shepherd;
I have everything I need.
PSALM 23:1

He will feed his flock like a shepherd. He will carry the lambs in his arms, holding them close to his heart. ISAIAH 40:11

I AM the Almighty, I AM WHO I AM.

God said, "I am who I am." EXODUS 3:14, TEV

I'll love you forever, whatever you do,
For nothing can separate my love from you.
I've loved everything that I made from the start.
My world and my people I hold in my heart.

Can anything ever separate us from Christ's love? I am convinced that nothing can ever separate us from his love. Death can't, and life can't . . . nothing in all creation will ever be able to separate us from the love of God that is revealed in Christ Jesus our Lord.
ROMANS 8:35, 38-39

What Is Prayer?

I have a few questions

to ask about prayer:

Can I talk to God

anytime, anywhere?

Are there special words

I should use when I pray?

Should I pray at nighttime

or during the day?

Does God hear the prayers

that I don't even speak?

How many times

may I pray in one week?

When I say my prayers,
should I bow down my head
And kneel on my knees
by the side of the bed?

When I first begin,
do I call God by name?
Should all of my prayers
be exactly the same?

Does God keep a list
of my prayers from before?
Will God give me all
that I ask for and more?

TT

Can I pray to God

when I'm angry inside?

Or would it be better

to go off and hide?

Can I pray for things

like a toy or a bike?

Should I pray for people

I don't even like?

TOYS
OP

Amen
Amém
Amén

Can I pray for something

and then pray again?

Why do we have to

end up with "amen"?

You want to know more
about how you should pray?
God's answer to that is,
"Terrific! Hooray!"

The Bible will tell you
just what you should know.
Let's see what it says to us—
ready, set, GO!

Talking to God

is a great thing to do.

And God's always ready

to listen to you.

You don't have to carefully
choose every word.
But you can be sure
that your prayers will be heard.

For even before
you have started to pray,
God already knows
what you're going to say!

Pray all you want to—

it's never too much.

Prayer is the way

you and God keep in touch.

Although you should always

say thank you and please,

You really don't have to

get down on your knees.

You can sit when you pray,

or lie down in your bed.

You can keep your eyes open

and stand on your head!

It's never a problem

however you start.

But God really wants you

to pray from your heart.

The more that you pray,

the more often you'll find

That prayers are all different,

not all the same kind.

There are prayers of thanksgiving

and also of praise,

Like, "Thank you, dear God,

for your wonderful ways!"

When you have done something

that you know is wrong,

Ask God to forgive you—

it doesn't take long.

If you're truly sorry,

then God will forgive.

And this will be true

for as long as you live.

When you are afraid

or you're grouchy or blue,

Then talking to God

is the best thing to do!

You can pray to the Lord
for whatever you need.
But praying for others
is special indeed.

Praying for someone

who isn't your friend

Is good for that person—

and *you, in the end.*

By praying for people
to know of God's love,
You're God's little blessing—
a gift from above.

God's answers to prayers

may come fast or come slow.

But God always answers,

and that much we know.

God never forgets

what you've asked for before.

But God doesn't mind

if you want to talk more.

Ending your prayer

with "amen" is a way

Of saying, "I've finished

my prayer now, okay?"

A prayer is a lot

like a telephone call.

You talk and you listen,

but that isn't all.

There's no busy signal—

you'll always get through.

And God never, ever

will hang up on you!

Bible References

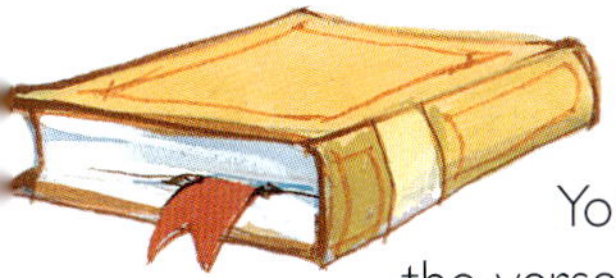

Here are some Bible verses to talk about as you read this book again with your child. You may want to open your Bible as you read the verses. This will help your little one understand that the answers in this poem come from God's Word, the Bible.

Talking to God is a great thing to do.
And God's always ready to listen to you.

Each morning I bring my requests to you. PSALM 5:3

Bend down, O Lord, and hear my prayer. PSALM 86:1

Jesus went to a mountain to pray, and he prayed to God all night. LUKE 6:12

You don't have to carefully choose every word.
But you can be sure that your prayers will be heard.

We don't even know what we should pray for, nor how we should pray. But the Holy Spirit prays for us with groanings that cannot be expressed in words. And the Father who knows all hearts knows what the Spirit is saying, for the Spirit pleads for us believers in harmony with God's own will.
ROMANS 8:26-27

For even before you have started to pray,
God already knows what you're going to say!

When you pray, . . . your Father knows exactly what you need even before you ask him! MATTHEW 6:7-8

Pray all you want to—it's never too much.
Prayer is the way you and God keep in touch.

Pray at all times and on every occasion. EPHESIANS 6:18

Keep on praying. 1 THESSALONIANS 5:17

Although you should always say thank you and please,
You really don't have to get down on your knees.

Pray about everything. Tell God what you need, and thank him for all he has done. PHILIPPIANS 4:6

You can sit when you pray, or lie down in your bed.
You can keep your eyes open and stand on your head!

When you pray, go away by yourself, shut the door behind you, and pray to your Father secretly. Then your Father, who knows all secrets, will reward you. MATTHEW 6:6

O Lord, you have examined my heart and know everything about me. You know when I sit down or stand up. You know my every thought when far away. PSALM 139:1-2

It's never a problem however you start.
But God really wants you to pray from your heart.

Devote yourselves to prayer with an alert mind and a thankful heart. COLOSSIANS 4:2

The more that you pray, the more often you'll find That prayers are all different, not all the same kind.

Pray like this: Our Father in heaven, may your name be honored. May your Kingdom come soon. May your will be done here on earth, just as it is in heaven. Give us our food for today, and forgive us our sins, just as we have forgiven those who have sinned against us. And don't let us yield to temptation, but deliver us from the evil one. MATTHEW 6:9-13

There are prayers of thanksgiving and also of praise, Like, "Thank you, dear God, for your wonderful ways!"

I will praise the Lord at all times. I will constantly speak his praises. PSALM 34:1

Shout joyful praises to God, all the earth! Sing about the glory of his name! PSALM 66:1-2

When you have done something that you know is wrong,
Ask God to forgive you—it doesn't take long.

If we confess our sins to [God], he is faithful and just to forgive us. I JOHN 1:9

If you're truly sorry, then God will forgive.
And this will be true for as long as you live.

If I had not confessed the sin in my heart, my Lord would not have listened. But God did listen! He paid attention to my prayer. PSALM 66:18-19

When you are afraid or you're grouchy or blue,
Then talking to God is the best thing to do!

I prayed to the Lord, and he answered me, freeing me from all my fears. PSALM 34:4

Be glad for all God is planning for you. Be patient in trouble, and always be prayerful. ROMANS 12:12

Tell God what you need, and thank him for all he has done. If you do this, you will experience God's peace, which is far more wonderful than the human mind can understand. His peace will guard your hearts and minds as you live in Christ Jesus. PHILIPPIANS 4:6-7

**You can pray to the Lord for whatever you need.
But praying for others is special indeed.**

Give all your worries and cares to God, for he cares about what happens to you. 1 PETER 5:7

Stay alert and be persistent in your prayers for all Christians everywhere. EPHESIANS 6:18

I urge you, first of all, to pray for all people. As you make your requests, plead for God's mercy upon them, and give thanks. 1 TIMOTHY 2:1

Praying for someone who isn't your friend
Is good for that person—*and* you, in the end.

But I say, love your enemies! Pray for those who persecute you! In that way, you will be acting as true children of your Father in heaven. MATTHEW 5:44-45

You can pray for anything, and if you believe, you will have it. But when you are praying, first forgive anyone you are holding a grudge against, so that your Father in heaven will forgive your sins, too. MARK 11:24-25

By praying for people to know of God's love,
You're God's little blessing—a gift from above.

The Lord . . . delights in the prayers of the upright. PROVERBS 15:8

Whatever you do or say, let it be as a representative of the Lord Jesus. COLOSSIANS 3:17

**God's answers to prayers may come fast or come slow.
But God always answers, and that much we know.**

Keep on asking, and you will be given what you ask for. Keep on looking, and you will find. Keep on knocking, and the door will be opened. LUKE 11:9

**God never forgets what you've asked for before.
But God doesn't mind if you want to talk more.**

I, the Lord, made you, and I will not forget to help you. ISAIAH 44:21

Pray about everything. PHILIPPIANS 4:6

**Ending your prayer with "amen" is a way
Of saying, "I've finished my prayer now, okay?"**

Blessed be the Lord, the God of Israel, from everlasting to everlasting! Let all the people say, "Amen!" Praise the Lord! PSALM 106:48

A prayer is a lot like a telephone call.
You talk and you listen, but that isn't all.

There's no busy signal—you'll always get through.
And God never, ever will hang up on you!

I am praying to you because I know you will answer, O God. PSALM 17:6

The Lord hears his people when they call to him for help. PSALM 34:17

What about Heaven?

I know that God loves me.

Of this there's no doubt.

But what about heaven?

What's that all about?

Is heaven a place

that is near or that's far?

Can I get to heaven

by boat or by car?

How will I find it?

Who'll show me the way?

Does heaven have nighttime?

And what about day?

Can I have a room

that is only for me?

Do I have to pay,

or can I stay for free?

Will I look the very

same way I do now?

Will everyone know

who I am? If so, how?

What food will I eat?

And what clothes will I wear?

When I get to heaven,

who else will be there?

Does heaven have mountains,

and trees I can climb?

What will I do there

with all of my time?

Is there enough space
for the animals, too?
Will there be some kind
of a heavenly zoo?

Since God is in heaven,

it has to be great.

Can I go there now,

or do I have to wait?

All questions have answers,
but some you won't learn
Till God says it's time
for his Son to return.
Your questions are good ones,
so let's dive right in
And see what the Bible says.
Ready? Begin!

Though heaven's a place

that you can't see from here,

It says in the Bible

that heaven is near.

You don't need to know

how to fly or to swim.

The way is with Jesus,

believing in him.

It always is daytime-

there never is night.

The light of God's love

will be shining so bright.

Jesus will give you

a room of your own,

With others nearby

so you won't feel alone.

Your body will change

so it's perfect and new,

And yet you will still be

the very same you.

But here's something different,
and this is no trick:
In heaven nobody
will ever get sick!
Our hurts will be healed,
and the deaf will all hear.

The blind will see clearly.

There's nothing to fear!

Everyone there

will be able to talk,

To sing and to dance,

and to run and to walk.

In heaven God serves you

the very best meal.

You'll never be hungry–

now that's a good deal!

The clothes that you'll wear

will be white and so clean;

In heaven you won't need

a washing machine!

Even the animals

won't want to fight;

They'll all get along–

they will not scratch or bite.

Though time has no ending,

you'll never get bored;

For thousands of years

seem like days to the Lord.

Heaven is full

of such beautiful things:

The music of millions of

angels who sing.

Rivers like crystal

and seas smooth as glass,

Emeralds glowing

like green springtime grass.

Mountains and jewels

of every type,

Trees full of fruits

that are juicy and ripe.

Sadness and pain

will be taken away;

Once you are there,

you'll be happy to stay.

All of God's children,

the young and the old,

Will gather together

on streets made of gold.

And then there will be

such a grand celebration

When heaven and earth

have become one creation!

Life will be perfect,

for heaven's the place

We'll see God, the Father

and Son, face-to-face.

For God will be there,

everywhere that you are;

And Jesus will shine

like a bright morning star.

Heaven is wonderful,

don't you agree?

It's simply the best place

we ever could be!

Bible References

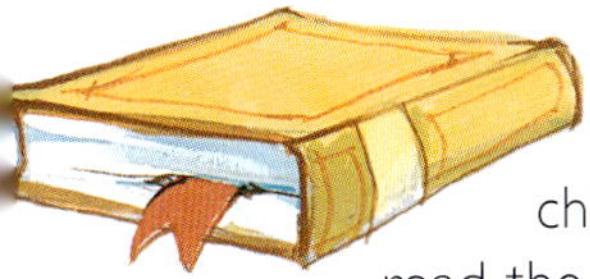

Here are some Bible verses to talk about as you read this book again with your child. You may want to open your Bible as you read the verses. This will help your little one understand that the answers in this poem come from God's Word, the Bible.

All questions have answers, but some you won't learn
Till God says it's time for his Son to return.
Your questions are good ones, so let's dive right in
And see what the Bible says. Ready? Begin!

> Everything that is now hidden or secret will eventually be brought to light. MARK 4:22

> All that I know now is partial and incomplete, but then I will know everything completely, just as God knows me now. 1 CORINTHIANS 13:12

**Though heaven's a place that you can't see from here,
It says in the Bible that heaven is near.**

Turn from your sins and turn to God, because the Kingdom of Heaven is near. MATTHEW 3:2

**You don't need to know how to fly or to swim.
The way is with Jesus, believing in him.**

For God so loved the world that he gave his only Son, so that everyone who believes in him will not perish but have eternal life. JOHN 3:16

I am the resurrection and the life. Those who believe in me, even though they die like everyone else, will live again. They are given eternal life for believing in me and will never perish. JOHN 11:25-26

When everything is ready, I will come and get you, so that you will always be with me where I am. JOHN 14:3

It always is daytime–there never is night.
The light of God's love will be shining so bright.

Its gates never close at the end of day because there is no night. REVELATION 21:25

There will be no night there—no need for lamps or sun—for the Lord God will shine on them. REVELATION 22:5

Jesus will give you a room of your own
With others nearby so you won't feel alone.

There are many rooms in my Father's home, and I am going to prepare a place for you. JOHN 14:2

Your body will change so it's perfect and new,
And yet you will still be the very same you.

We, too, wait anxiously for that day when God will give us our full rights as his children, including the new bodies he has promised us. ROMANS 8:23

There are bodies in the heavens, and there are bodies on earth. The glory of the heavenly bodies is different from the beauty of the earthly bodies.
1 CORINTHIANS 15:40

We grow weary in our present bodies, and we long for the day when we will put on our heavenly bodies like new clothing. For we will not be spirits without bodies, but we will put on new heavenly bodies.
2 CORINTHIANS 5:2-3

But here's something different, and this is no trick:
In heaven nobody will ever get sick!

Our earthly bodies . . . will be different when they are resurrected, for they will never die. They are natural human bodies now, but when they are raised, they will be spiritual bodies. 1 CORINTHIANS 15:42, 44

Our hurts will be healed, and the deaf will all hear.
The blind will see clearly. There's nothing to fear!

In that day deaf people will hear words read from a book, and blind people will see through the gloom and darkness. ISAIAH 29:18

Our perishable earthly bodies must be transformed into heavenly bodies that will never die. 1 CORINTHIANS 15:53

The troubles we see will soon be over. 2 CORINTHIANS 4:18

Everyone there will be able to talk,
To sing and to dance, and to run and to walk.

The people of God will sing a song of joy. ISAIAH 30:29

Those who wait on the Lord will find new strength. They will fly high on wings like eagles. They will run and not grow weary. They will walk and not faint. ISAIAH 40:31

In heaven God serves you the very best meal.
You'll never be hungry–now that's a good deal!

The Lord Almighty will spread a wonderful feast for everyone around the world. It will be a delicious feast of good food. ISAIAH 25:6

I will come in, and we will share a meal as friends. REVELATION 3:20

They will never again be hungry or thirsty. REVELATION 7:16

The clothes that you'll wear will be white and so clean;
In heaven you won't need a washing machine!

All who are victorious will be clothed in white.
REVELATION 3:5

They were clothed in white and held palm branches in their hands. REVELATION 7:9

Even the animals won't want to fight;
They'll all get along–they will not scratch or bite.

In that day the wolf and the lamb will live together; the leopard and the goat will be at peace. Calves and yearlings will be safe among lions. . . . The cattle will graze among bears. Cubs and calves will lie down together. And lions will eat grass as the livestock do. ISAIAH 11:6-7

Though time has no ending, you'll never get bored;
For thousands of years seem like days to the Lord.

For you, a thousand years are as yesterday! They are like a few hours! PSALM 90:4

A day is like a thousand years to the Lord, and a thousand years is like a day. 2 PETER 3:8

Heaven is full of such beautiful things:
The music of millions of angels who sing.

Then I looked again, and I heard the singing of thousands and millions of angels around the throne and the living beings and the elders. REVELATION 5:11

Rivers like crystal and seas smooth as glass,
Emeralds glowing like green springtime grass.

The glow of an emerald circled his throne like a rainbow. REVELATION 4:3

In front of the throne was a shiny sea of glass. REVELATION 4:6

The angel showed me a pure river with the water of life, clear as crystal. REVELATION 22:1

Mountains and jewels of every type,
Trees full of fruits that are juicy and ripe.

Nothing will hurt or destroy in all my holy mountain. ISAIAH 11:9

He took me in spirit to a great, high mountain.
REVELATION 21:10

The wall of the city was built on foundation stones inlaid with twelve gems: the first was jasper, the second sapphire, the third agate, the fourth emerald, the fifth onyx, the sixth carnelian, the seventh chrysolite, the eighth beryl, the ninth topaz, the tenth chrysoprase, the eleventh jacinth, the twelfth amethyst.
REVELATION 21:19-20

On each side of the river grew a tree of life, bearing twelve crops of fruit, with a fresh crop each month.
REVELATION 22:2

Sadness and pain will be taken away;
Once you are there, you'll be happy to stay.

The Sovereign Lord will wipe away all tears. ISAIAH 25:8

Sorrow and mourning will disappear, and they will be overcome with joy and gladness. ISAIAH 51:11

He will remove all of their sorrows, and there will be no more death or sorrow or crying or pain.
REVELATION 21:4

All of God's children, the young and the old,
Will gather together on streets made of gold.

All who are victorious will inherit all these blessings, and I will be their God, and they will be my children.
REVELATION 21:7

The main street was pure gold,
as clear as glass.
REVELATION 21:21

And then there will be such a grand celebration
When heaven and earth have become one creation!

All creation anticipates the day when it will join God's children in glorious freedom from death and decay. ROMANS 8:21

Then I saw a new heaven and a new earth, for the old heaven and the old earth had disappeared. REVELATION 21:1

Life will be perfect, for heaven's the place
We'll see God, the Father and Son, face-to-face.

Nothing evil will be allowed to enter. REVELATION 21:27

Now we see things imperfectly as in a poor mirror, but then we will see everything with perfect clarity. 1 CORINTHIANS 13:12

The throne of God and of the Lamb will be there, and his servants will worship him. And they will see his face. REVELATION 22:3-4

For God will be there, everywhere that you are;
And Jesus will shine like a bright morning star.

I am the bright morning star. REVELATION 22:16

Heaven is wonderful, don't you agree?
It's simply the best place we ever could be!

Don't be troubled. You trust God, now trust in me. JOHN 14:1

The joys to come will last forever. 2 CORINTHIANS 4:18

The old world and its evils are gone forever. REVELATION 21:4

Are Angels Real?

I've heard there are angels.

Oh, can it be true?

Are angels for real?

And just what do they do?

Do I have an angel

that looks after me?

Can I talk to angels?

Can they hear and see?

C.K.
+
JG

Will angels be glad

if I do what is right?

MAIN
STO

Does God tuck them into

their cloud beds at night?

Do angels wear slippers
or sandals or shoes?
I know I'd go barefoot
if I got to choose!

Do angels have power?

Are they very strong?

If I am afraid,

will they sing me a song?

Do angels have wings,

and can all of them fly?

Do angels grow older,

and then do they die?

Are there many angels,

or only a few?

When I go to heaven,

can I be one too?

Are angels for real?
There is no need to guess.
The Bible assures us
the answer is yes!

So, who made the angels?
Well, God did, that's who!
And God gives the angels
their own jobs to do.

When God has a message,

he often will use

An angel to bring us

the wonderful news.

The angels serve God

in their own special ways

And then give to God

all the glory and praise.

You can't always see them,

but this you should know:

The angels are with you

wherever you go.

Yet when you have something

important to say,

It's God, not the angels,

to whom you should pray.

Tell God that you're sorry
for doing what's wrong.
Then all of the angels
will sing a glad song!

Elena

Angels are spirits–

they don't need to sleep.

God never says, "Quiet!

Now don't make a peep!"

As far as what angels
might wear for their clothes,
They dress up in light
from their head to their toes!

Their power is used

to obey God's commands.

They even can hold back

the wind with their hands!

Though angels are mighty
and strong, you will find
That angels are also
quite gentle and kind.

When you are afraid,

here is what you can do:

Imagine that angels

are singing to you.

Elena

Angels are speedy,

and this is no lie—

They move place to place

in the blink of an eye.

Now, here is another

remarkable thing:

All angels can fly,

but they don't all need wings!

There may be some angels
with no wings, it's true,
While some may have six,
and still others have two.

Angels aren't born,
and they never grow old.
They never get married,
from what we are told.

Angels don't die,
though that seems rather odd,
For they are already
in heaven with God.

Just how many are there?

What is the amount?

Thousands and millions–

too many to count!

Now, maybe you think
it would be lots of fun
To be a real angel
when this life is done.

We won't become angels,
but that is OK.
We'll all be together
in heaven someday.

Until that time comes,

here's a word of advice:

Treat everyone kindly,
and try to be nice.

If you share God's love
as we're all meant to do,
You just might be helping
an angel out too!

Bible References

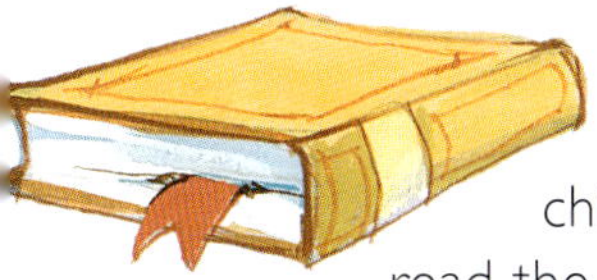

Here are some Bible verses to talk about as you read this book again with your child. You may want to open your Bible as you read the verses. This will help your little one understand that the answers in this poem come from God's Word, the Bible.

Are angels for real? There is no need to guess.
The Bible assures us the answer is yes!
So, who made the angels? Well, God did, that's who!
And God gives the angels their own jobs to do.

Christ is the one through whom God created everything in heaven and earth. He made the things we can see and the things we can't see. COLOSSIANS 1:16

Praise the Lord, you angels of his, you mighty creatures who carry out his plans, listening for each of his commands. Yes, praise the Lord, you armies of angels who serve him and do his will! PSALM 103:20-21

When God has a message, he often will use
An angel to bring us the wonderful news.

The angel said [to Zechariah], "I am Gabriel! I stand in the very presence of God. It was he who sent me to bring you this good news!" LUKE 1:19

God sent the angel Gabriel to Nazareth. . . . "[Mary,] God has decided to bless you!" LUKE 1:26, 30

An angel of the Lord appeared among [the shepherds]. . . . "I bring you good news of great joy for everyone!" LUKE 2:9-10

The angels serve God in their own special ways
And then give to God all the glory and praise.

In a great chorus they sang, "Holy, holy, holy is the Lord Almighty! The whole earth is filled with his glory!" The glorious singing shook the Temple to its foundations, and the entire sanctuary was filled with smoke. ISAIAH 6:3-4

When he presented his honored Son to the world, God said, "Let all the angels of God worship him." HEBREWS 1:6

You can't always see them, but this you should know:
The angels are with you wherever you go.

He orders his angels to protect you wherever you go. They will hold you with their hands to keep you from striking your foot on a stone. PSALM 91:11-12

Gabriel roused me with a touch and helped me to my feet. DANIEL 8:18

An angel of the Lord came at night, opened the gates of the jail, and brought [the apostles] out. ACTS 5:19

Yet when you have something important to say,
It's God, not the angels, to whom you should pray.

Don't let anyone say you must worship angels, even though they say they have had visions about this. COLOSSIANS 2:18

The angel said to me, . . . "These are true words that come from God." Then I fell down at his feet to worship him, but he said, "No, don't worship me. For I am a servant of God, just like you and other believers who testify of their faith in Jesus. Worship God." REVELATION 19:9-10

Tell God that you're sorry for doing what's wrong.
Then all of the angels will sing a glad song!

There is joy in the presence of God's angels when even one sinner repents. LUKE 15:10

Angels are spirits—they don't need to sleep.
God never says, "Quiet! Now don't make a peep!"

As [Jacob] slept, he dreamed of a stairway that reached from earth to heaven. And he saw the angels of God going up and down on it. GENESIS 28:12

Last night an angel of the God to whom I belong and whom I serve stood beside me, and he said, "Don't be afraid, Paul." ACTS 27:23-24

Angels are only servants. They are spirits sent from God to care for those who will receive salvation. HEBREWS 1:14

**As far as what angels might wear for their clothes,
They dress up in light from their head to their toes!**

Suddenly there was a great earthquake, because an angel of the Lord came down from heaven and rolled aside the stone and sat on it. His face shone like lightning, and his clothing was as white as snow. Matthew 28:2-3

Suddenly, there was a bright light in the cell, and an angel of the Lord stood before Peter. Acts 12:7

Then I saw another mighty angel coming down from heaven, surrounded by a cloud, with a rainbow over his head. His face shone like the sun, and his feet were like pillars of fire. Revelation 10:1

Their power is used to obey God's commands.
They even can hold back the wind with their hands!

Then I saw four angels standing at the four corners of the earth, holding back the four winds from blowing upon the earth. REVELATION 7:1

After all this I saw another angel come down from heaven with great authority, and the earth grew bright with his splendor. REVELATION 18:1

Though angels are mighty and strong, you will find
That angels are also quite gentle and kind.

[Elijah] lay down and slept under the broom tree. But as he was sleeping, an angel touched him and told him, "Get up and eat!" . . . Then the angel of the Lord came again and touched him and said, "Get up and eat some more, for there is a long journey ahead of you." I KINGS 19:5, 7

If a special messenger from heaven is there to intercede for a person, to declare that he is upright, God will be gracious and say, "Set him free." JOB 33:23-24

When you are afraid, here is what you can do:
Imagine that angels are singing to you.

[The shepherds] were terribly frightened, but the angel reassured them. "Don't be afraid!" he said. "I bring you good news of great joy for everyone! . . ." Suddenly, the angel was joined by a vast host of others—the armies of heaven—praising God: "Glory to God in the highest heaven, and peace on earth to all whom God favors."
LUKE 2:9-10, 13-14

The angel spoke to the women [at the tomb]. "Don't be afraid!" he said. "I know you are looking for Jesus, who was crucified. He isn't here! He has been raised from the dead, just as he said would happen." MATTHEW 28:5-6

Angels are speedy, and this is no lie–
They move place to place in the blink of an eye.

God calls his angels "messengers swift as the wind, and servants made of flaming fire." HEBREWS 1:7

I saw another angel flying through the heavens, carrying the everlasting Good News to preach to the people who belong to this world—to every nation, tribe, language, and people. REVELATION 14:6

Now, here is another remarkable thing:
All angels can fly, but they don't all need wings!
There may be some angels with no wings, it's true,
While some may have six, and still others have two.

[An angel appeared as a man to Samson's parents before their baby was born:] Manoah ran back with his wife and asked, "Are you the man who talked to my wife?" . . . Manoah finally realized it was the angel of the Lord. JUDGES 13:11, 21

[Isaiah saw angels called seraphim:] Hovering around [the Lord] were mighty seraphim, each with six wings. ISAIAH 6:2

[Ezekiel saw angels called cherubim:] The moving wings of the cherubim sounded like the voice of God Almighty. EZEKIEL 10:5

[Gold cherubim were placed in Solomon's Temple:] Solomon made two figures shaped like cherubim and overlaid them with gold. . . . One wing of the first figure . . . touched the Temple wall. The other wing . . . touched one of the wings of the second figure. 2 CHRONICLES 3:10-11

Angels aren't born, and they never grow old.
They never get married, from what we are told.
Angels don't die, though that seems rather odd,
For they are already in heaven with God.

Praise him, all his angels! Praise him, all the armies of heaven! PSALM 148:2

Jesus replied, ". . . When the dead rise, they won't be married. They will be like the angels in heaven." MARK 12:24-25

Just how many are there? What is the amount?
Thousands and millions—too many to count!

I looked again, and I heard the singing of thousands and millions of angels around the throne and the living beings and the elders. REVELATION 5:11

Now, maybe you think it would be lots of fun
To be a real angel when this life is done.
We won't become angels, but that is OK.
We'll all be together in heaven someday.

He will send forth his angels to gather together his chosen ones from all over the world—from the farthest ends of the earth and heaven. MARK 13:27

You have come to Mount Zion, to the city of the living God, the heavenly Jerusalem, and to thousands of angels in joyful assembly. HEBREWS 12:22

Until that time comes, here's a word of advice:
Treat everyone kindly, and try to be nice.
If you share God's love as we're all meant to do,
You just might be helping an angel out too!

Don't forget to show hospitality to strangers, for some who have done this have entertained angels without realizing it! HEBREWS 13:2

About the Author

Kathleen Long Bostrom is the author of seven Little Blessings books. Two are board books, and five have poetic questions based on actual questions from "little blessings" she has known. She has also written another book of verse, *The World That God Made*, plus numerous newspaper and magazine articles, and several prize-winning sermons.

Kathy earned a doctor of ministry in preaching degree from McCormick Theological Seminary in Chicago, Illinois, and both a master of arts in Christian education and a master of divinity degree from Princeton Theological Seminary. She also has a bachelor of arts degree in psychology from California State University, Long Beach, California.

Wildwood, Illinois, is where Kathy and her husband, Greg, live with their three children, Christopher, Amy, and David. Kathy and Greg serve as co-pastors of the Wildwood Presbyterian Church.

About the Illustrator

Elena Kucharik, well-known Care Bears artist, has created the Little Blessings characters, which appear in the Little Blessings line of products for young children and their families.

Born in Cleveland, Ohio, Elena received a bachelor of fine arts degree in commercial art at Kent State University. After graduation she worked as a greeting card artist and art director at American Greetings Corporation in Cleveland.

For the past 25 years Elena has been a freelance illustrator. During this time she was the lead artist and developer of Care Bears, as well as a designer and illustrator for major corporations and publishers. For the past 10 years Elena has been focusing her talents on illustrations for children's books.

Elena and her husband live in Madison, Connecticut, and have two grown daughters.